Sacred Light Oracle

Ascension cards for the spiritual seeker

ANNA STARK

Illustrated by Selena Moon

ROCKPOOL

A Rockpool book
PO Box 252
Summer Hill
NSW 2130
Australia

rockpoolpublishing.com

Follow us! **f** **◎** rockpoolpublishing
Tag your images with #rockpoolpublishing

ISBN: 9781925946260

Published in 2021 by Rockpool Publishing
Copyright text © Anna Stark 2021
Copyright images © Selena Moon 2021
Copyright design © Rockpool Publishing 2021

Design by Sara Lindberg, Rockpool Publishing
Edited by Lisa Macken

Printed and bound in China
10 9 8 7 6 5 4 3 2

Contents

ACKNOWLEDGEMENTS   1

INTRODUCTION   3

HOW TO USE THE CARDS   4

SACRED LIGHT ORACLE CARDS   15

1. Angelic realms 16
2. Antakarana 18
3. Archangel Michael 20
4. Ascension flame 22
5. Cathedral of light 24
6. Celestial channel 26
7. Consciousness 28
8. Cosmic gateway 30
9. Cosmic wave 32
10. Crystal kingdom 34
11. Dharma wheel 36
12. Divine creation 38
13. Energy attachments 40
14. Energy medicine 42
15. Galactic vibration 44
16. Golden light ray 46
17. Inner oracle 48
18. Language of light 50
19. Light activation 52

20. Light body 54

21. Light seeker 56

22. Lord Melchizedek 58

23. Magical alchemy 60

24. Past life 62

25. Power of presence 64

26. Sacred space 66

27. Scales of karma 68

28. Soul family 70

29. Sphere of light 72

30. Spirit guides 74

31. Temple of Mary 76

32. Temple secrets 78

33. Tibetan fire serpent 80

34. Universal Merkabah 82

35. Violet fire 84

36. Well-being 86

ABOUT THE AUTHOR   88

ABOUT THE ILLUSTRATOR   90

OTHER PUBLICATIONS   92

Acknowledgements

My primary focus with the creation of these cards was to provide people with ascension tools to raise their personal vibration. The human experience is all about learning and evolving into our authenticity, and it is with my heart that this deck was born to support the sacred light of our soul. This guide was designed to help you on your personal quest to connect with the higher realms of light, to converse with the spiritual hierarchy on a personal level.

If you have just awakened your intuition, you are going on a blessed self-journey that will bring you closer to your divine purpose and spiritual self.

It is with deep gratitude and love that I thank my life partner and husband Ian for his unwavering support through the creation of *Sacred Light Oracle*, and to my darling daughter whose rainbow spirit has taught me so much already on how to keep all our lights shining.

Thank you, Allen and Jill, for your continued support and friendship: my teachers past and present and those in the realm of spirit. May you continue to light the path for global change, awakening love and acceptance across this beautiful planet.

Most importantly, a big heartfelt thank you to the artist and to Lisa Hanrahan, Paul Dennett and the beautiful souls at Rockpool Publishing for their patience and professionalism, allowing the birthing of these ascension cards to help humanity.

Your soul has brought you to this deck for a reason. No matter your connection to spirit, earth, animals, stars or to source, you will find tools that will bring you closer to your own divine path and union with the universe, where you can live with authenticity and love.

This oracle is dedicated to all those seeking to raise their vibration and improve their life and connection with the universe. Through your soul's intentions, you can live a loving, blessed and powerful life!

Let your soul and intuition guide you.

In love,

Anna

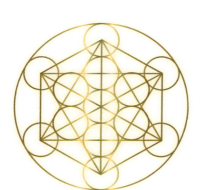

Introduction

The *Sacred Light Oracle* is designed to support your intuitive growth and awareness of your deep connection within the universe. The deck consists of 36 cards that blend messages from the ascended masters and spiritual hierarchy and intuitive actions with guidance from the soul, and hold spiritual and healing messages. Every card has an associated ascension master, crystal and affirmation that is aligned to support you in shifting your vibration to search for ascension. The specific messages included with each card have been directly channelled to support you personally.

To elevate your spiritual vibration and understanding I suggest you connect to different members of the earthly ascension team when they make themselves appear to you. Work with their 100 per cent pure light aspects to hear their messages of support as you raise your love light to new heights.

Use the energy of *Sacred Light Oracle* during oracle readings, meditation, daily and nightly affirmations, mirror work and creative inspiration. Use *Sacred Light Oracle* along with *Sacred Spirit Reading Cards* or *Sacred Power Reading Cards* for deeper insight and intuitive readings. I strongly recommend you record your readings, meditations and soul's messages in a journal for reflection and to monitor your healing progress and other intuitive insights.

How to use the cards

Any divinatory or healing tool you use is an energetic extension of yourself. The *Sacred Light Oracle* has been lovingly created to encourage your natural intuition, support your self-awareness, compliment self-healing and guide your spirit towards ascension. You will also find ascension masters and crystal associations to support your energy and spiritual work. The cards can be used in a traditional oracle or tarot reading format in simple or elaborate spreads to answer specific questions or give deep insight. Use the cards as spiritual prompts to grow your intuitive skills and give detailed readings.

You may find meaning in hidden symbols, colours, astrological influences, shapes and numbers within these cards. Let yourself be guided by these messages from your angels, guides and consciousness helpers to deliver a personalised message about the subject, issue or experience you are seeking guidance on.

Connecting with your deck

It is essential you make your cards as clear as possible to receive the best, reliable and most accurate information possible. Holding the deck in your hands, touch each card individually, turning them over and viewing each picture. This will connect you to each card before you begin working with them, infusing them with your unique vibration.

Hold the cards near your heart space and feel, sense or know that you are connecting with them on this level. Think about their purpose for you. What is your intention for this deck? What are you seeking from it? Hold these thoughts and any other intentions you have for them in your mind and recite this mantra, or your own, to activate and ground your cards:

'It is with my soul's highest intention that all readings bring clear, accurate and divine guidance and healing. I ask that messages be delivered with 100 per cent pure light consciousness with love, clarity and confidence as I am a clear divine channel.'

Tip: to keep your cards clear and energised between sessions, wrap them in a special cloth of your choosing and place a piece of clear quartz crystal with your deck. This will set the tone for clear, accurate and decisive readings.

Healing and meditation

Prepare your meditation space. Make yourself comfortable, take a few deep breaths in and release anything that doesn't need to be here in this moment. Keeping your palms facing upward, let your breath find its natural rhythm. Focus on an issue or what you would like to heal in your life.

When you are ready, select a card. Hold the card in front of you and focus on the image, connecting with the energy integrated within the card. Hold this image in your mind's eye, allowing your mind, body and soul to receive. Hold the space for as long as you intuit is necessary or until you feel a shift occur. Take note of any thoughts, feelings and images that occur and acknowledge them. This will give you greater insight into the issue in question. Keep a journal of your experiences to record your progress.

Oracle readings

Let go of any expectation you have on an outcome. Think of something you would like an answer to: it may be an issue you are facing, an experience you have just been through or an event coming up. If you are giving a reading to someone else, ask them to think of or ask a question. As you shuffle the cards, your spirit helpers will bring the right cards forward to answer these questions.

Card of the day

When using the cards as a healing tool, it is strongly encouraged that you begin a daily journal to aid in personal reflection. Simply select a card at the beginning of the day and meditate on the image. Write down your thoughts, feelings and other information that arises during this time. Check the meaning and add it to your journal.

One-card reading

Hold your deck and ask a question in your mind or out loud. If you don't have a specific question, ask your cards: *'What message do you have for me today?'*, *'What do I need to know right now?'*, *'Which ascension master can help me right now?'* or *'What crystal can I work with now to improve my situation?'* Choose a single card that should help you with an answer.

The layout and design of *Sacred Light Oracle* encourages energetic action for ascension. Asking questions such as these will assist you in incorporating energy work, crystal therapy, angelic assistance and intuitive guidance.

Take action spread

Card 1: **current situation –** your current position in life.

Card 2: **challenge –** something from the past that is still influencing you.

Card 3: **action –** the possible outcome or how to move forward based on current events.

Sacred light spread

Card 1: represents the person currently asking the question; it is the centre of the reading.

Card 2: the past issues impacting the current vibrational situation.

Card 3: current or near-future challenges affecting the questioner's vibration.

Card 4: the influences affecting the questioner's ability to connect clearly to consciousness.

Card 5: how to support your spiritual growth.

Card 6: how to attract more light into this situation.

Card 7: which action can balance the questioner.

Card 8: which ascension master can help bring further healing, clarity and ascension.

Seven Ray ascension light spread

This spread will bring forth direct messages from each of the Seven Rays, communicating with you how you can elevate your ascension and love light through each individual ray.

Card 1: .First Ray – how to improve courage, power, faith and self-reliance.

Card 2: Second Ray – how to raise knowledge, education, emotion and illumination.

Card 3: Third Ray – how to communicate divine love, creative expression, artistry and compassion.

Card 4: Fourth Ray – how to achieve self-discipline, ascension and mastery.

Card 5: Fifth Ray – your relationship with health, truth, philosophy and science.

Card 6: Sixth Ray – your level of communion with service, peace and ministration.

Card 7: Seventh Ray – how you can create transmutation, freedom, alchemy and divine ritual.

Card 8: sacred fire – a timely message from Ascended Master Maha Chohan.

Card 9: soul message – what your soul needs you to know right now.

The ascension masters

Archangels, ascended masters and galactic healers have been included within the extended card meanings in this deck. Those included have been the most significant for me personally on my ascension journey, although all ascension masters are willing to share their healing energy if you ask them with respect, and all archangels are healers. All you need to do is request their energy be shared with you on a conscious and physical level for the appropriate length of healing time.

Each card meaning has an ascension master suggestion that resonates with the specific card. I have included archangels, ascended masters, galactic masters and earth guardians. The masters listed are a guide only, as there are many more ascension masters with whom you can connect as they receive their celestial graduation to aid humanity. You can work with each one or gently and lovingly ask to work with the most appropriate for you at that moment.

How you choose to personally connect with these light beings is up to you. A helpful suggestion is to clear and set your sacred space as you would for meditation, keeping your palms facing upwards or in a self-healing hand position over the heart chakra and solar plexus.

Crystal healing

All crystals have their own beautiful and loving energy. Within the guidebook's extended card meanings you will find a crystal suggestion. The crystals included in this deck are usually readily available, with perhaps a few being rare. Directly associated with each card, they are high vibrational crystals that will support healing and ascension practice. While they are a guide only, I encourage you to explore all crystal energy as you walk the path of ascension. Let your intuition guide you to explore the crystal realm.

To incorporate crystalline energy into your readings or practice and achieve the most benefits, keep these associated crystals around your person, aura or desired space. If you are an experienced crystal therapist you may consider using these suggestions in your readings, crystal grids or personal sessions.

Important note: always keep your crystals cleansed before placing them on your body or wearing or incorporating them into your healing practice.

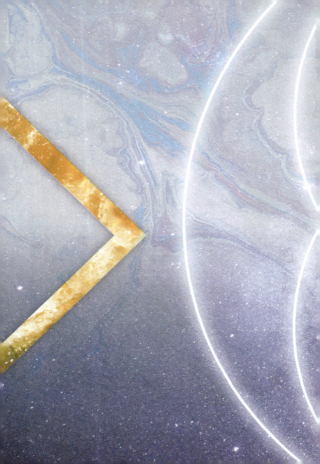

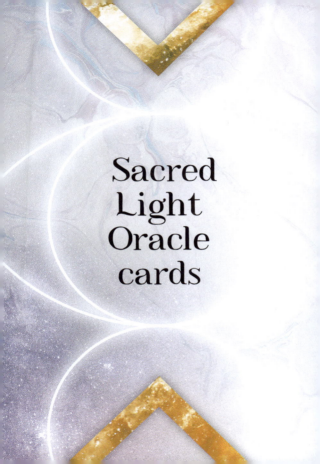

Sacred
Light
Oracle
cards

A team effort. Charity. Validation. Patience.

1 Angelic realms

A team effort. Charity. Validation. Patience.

The keepers of the angelic realm are the angelic hierarchy. They are conduits for healing energy, spirit messengers, awakenings and deep spiritual insights. Speaking to you constantly, they are protectors and healers who can help you in any area of your life. Assisting in this collaboration, Archangel Metatron radiates in God light and holds the sacred geometric cube that connects all living creatures and energies to the divine.

Taking personal responsibility will ensure a cohesive angelic relationship. Working with the loving angelic realm is Paul the Venetian from the Third Ray. The union between the physical and divine is created by surrendering with gratitude and an open heart. Connect to the artist within you to express your divine light.

Being a conscious creator, you have the power to liberate your soul so you can ascend your spirit. Charitable actions should be expressed with compassion instead of sympathy; only then can you receive and surround others with the beautiful light and love that is open to all in its purest element.

Loving Ascension Master Paul the Venetian is signalling your attention to ask you to be more compassionate in your life with your friends, family and colleagues, understanding that you are all on a separate journey. Light flashes, feathers and unusual animal interactions have messages for you from the angelic realm. You have angelic support.

'The time is now. Express your heart with full freedom. Chase your heart.'

– ASCENDED MASTER PAUL THE VENETIAN

Sacred crystal: celestite

Affirmation: *'I surrender my fear and open my heart to gratitude.'*

2 Antakarana

Crossing the rainbow bridge.
Resurrection. Coming full circle.

The antakarana forms a connection between your intelligent mind and the higher levels of your perception and consciousness. Identified as the source of supreme thinking, the antakarana is mind, soul, heart or conscience. An ancient symbol used for spiritual healing, it can amplify the healing of any technique or practice you choose to use in your life. Meditation, massage, breathing exercises, hypnosis, energy work, traditional medicine and medical practices will enhance the healing potential of your chosen method.

Antakarana is a Sanskrit word for 'rainbow bridge'. Coming full circle, this is a time for those who are ready to cross this rainbow bridge and send their spirit home. Surround them with love and a peaceful environment to ease their transition. Moments of serendipity will leave you inspired.

Acknowledge and process a plan for moving forward and you will finally put to rest old issues or experiences that have up until now exhausted you. All your perceived problems will feel overwhelming, and it will almost seem like there is no light at the end of the tunnel from your circumstances.

Ascension Master Jesus asks you to see the hidden blessings in your conflicts and traumas. Overwhelming feelings have the potential to consume you now: feelings of anxiety, grief, fear and a need for control in your life will create mountains for you to climb. Apply a different mindset to take small steps to lighten your soul and unburden your spirit.

'My love knows no bounds. I am endless.'

– ASCENDED MASTER JESUS

Sacred crystal: elestial quartz

Affirmation: *'My energy is amplified through positive action. My heart is full.'*

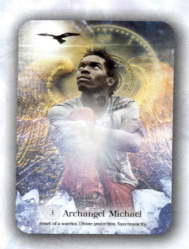

3 Archangel Michael
Heart of a warrior. Divine protection. Synchronicity.

3 Archangel Michael

Heart of a warrior. Divine protection. Synchronicity.

The most respected angel in all faiths, scriptures and spiritual traditions, Archangel Michael commands the legions of guardian angels on the First Ray. Aligned with faith and in the will of God, Archangel Michael assists souls that are trapped or lost or bound by fear to the astral plane.

Archangel Michael can help you release lower and toxic energies such as fear and worry so you can open yourself to experience love and connection with the purity of the angelic realm. Ready to battle in an instant, Archangel

Michael guides you to a clearer path, self-connection and personal strength. If you are lacking faith in your future and feeling unable to trust your inner thoughts or intuitive senses, ask the angels for assistance.

Intuitively, Archangel Michael initiates experiences with spirit, helping you to connect with and awaken to your intuitive senses. Spiritual experiences, serendipity and angel numbers and sequences are all around now. Be vigilant, as the signs are everywhere.

Ascension guide Archangel Michael is guiding you to find passion and purpose in life. Listening to your inner voice and acknowledging any fear you have about your future will lead you closer to a positive life path. You are encouraged at this time to listen more to yourself, to your heart and into your sense of knowing so you may walk vibrantly on a golden path with purpose. Mediumship and spirit talking are supported now. Remove any barriers that stop you from hearing spirit messages.

'May your strength return in the flight of your own courage.'

– *ARCHANGEL MICHAEL*

Sacred crystal: sapphire

Affirmation: *'My path is clear. I am divinely guided and protected.'*

4 Ascension flame

**Liberation. A sense of greater purpose.
High expectations.**

The ascension flame is strongest in the temples of Luxor, Egypt and can be called on to raise your energetic vibration to a higher state of knowing and consciousness. In order to accept and integrate the ascension flame within your four body systems – mental, physical, spiritual and emotional – challenges and outdated belief patterns *must* be broken.

In order to achieve a rise in ascension you will be provided with some of the greatest challenges that, accordingly, align to your karmic blueprint. During these times, enlightenment from the lessons learned will raise your vibration to a higher level. The key is to move forward with an enlightened wisdom.

Master of the ascension temple Serapis Bey holds the ascension flame on the Fourth Ray of purity if you are ready to conquer your own misguidance, distorted energies and belief programs. Set real-time expectations and discipline your mind to create achievable outcomes and a state of clear consciousness.

Ascended Master Serapis Bey is guiding you through a challenging experience. Deliberate attempts by others to engage emotional responses, or 'gaslighting', will only prove you have moved on from the past. Interests in ancient symbols, hieroglyphs, the ancient Egyptians, pyramids and astrology all signify that you are ready to ascend and let go of old energy. Begin and continue your ascension with self-improvement goals.

'Be all that you can be despite your perceived misgivings. Grow knowledge over power.'

– *ASCENDED MASTER SERAPIS BEY*

Sacred crystal: cacoxenite

Affirmation: *'I can confront anything before me. I am a powerful beacon of light.'*

5 Cathedral of light

Stubborn attitudes.
Extending the olive branch. Artistry.

A cathedral is a large and beautiful place of worship often filled with beautiful stained glass windows, ancient architecture, historical religious figures and sacred rituals. The cathedral of light is just as you might imagine: a beautiful building filled with glorious colours resonating at pure vibrational light energy, lifting the heaviest and darkest of energies when you sit within its beautiful space.

Through the void, the cathedral of light is accessible through meditation and in deep trance states. Surrounded by universal light codes, its high energy and creative coding encourages ingenuity, magical inspiration and originality. The cathedral of light brings new life by adjusting conservative views and beliefs.

The Grecian beauty and green ray lady master Pallas Athena directs those who choose to enter to purify, recharge and illuminate areas that have been previously hidden. Initiating this energetic dispersion refracts remnants of dense lower energy into sacred light. It is simply magical.

Ascended Master Pallas Athena asks you to embrace your inner warrior. Extend the olive branch before you dig in and defend your territories. Lower energies and thought forms that have become a constant disruption to your everyday routines must be attacked head on. Interests in mediaeval cathedrals and sacred and ancient architecture highlight a need to visit these sacred spaces and the cathedral of light, allowing the refractions of its beauty to permeate your aura.

'Beauty may shine first but light will always shine the brightest.'

– ASCENDED MASTER PALLAS ATHENA

Sacred crystal: danburite

Affirmation: *'My light is radiant. My body removes toxins with ease and comfort.'*

6 Celestial channel

Hidden beauty. Remaining optimistic. Staying neutral.

Being a clear celestial channel requires peace of spirit. Constant interruptions and anxieties about employment and family commitments consume your mind, when instead you really want to nurture your soul and put your feet up and relax. As a channel for celestial connections, every effort should be made to be free from fear, anxiety or lower-based energies as energetic clouds make interpretations difficult.

With magic and mystery, Lady Sara holds the sacred keys to the Akashic temple. Her earthly mission is to provide support and direction for any future paths, teaching the souls of the earth how to surrender to the present and feel satisfied and content in life. See the blessing in what you have right now even though you may be afraid of missing out.

Ascension Master Lady Sara asks you to remember the polarity of being. You must honour the light and shadow aspects within yourself as they are a part of you; you can learn from both aspects as a clear celestial channel and must make peace with them to create your future path.

You have and will always be a celestial channel of pure intent. Maintain clear neutrality while channelling to create optimum reception. Lady Sara sees the beauty that hides in messy and confronting situations, and suggests you reflect on the past but move forward with gratitude and optimism. Just like the sun and the moon, these energetic celestials have their own time to shine.

'The sun and the moon exist in the same cycles, like the shadows in the light.'

– *ASCENSION MASTER LADY SARA*

Sacred crystal: hiddenite

Affirmation: *'I learn through rising challenges. My soul embraces these experiences with success.'*

7 Consciousness
Self-awareness. Personal realisations. Prejudice.

7 Consciousness

Self-awareness. Personal realisations. Prejudice.

The divine invisible thread of consciousness connects you with everyone else. It is so strong it enables links and connections with others through consciousness instantaneously. Knowing who was calling you, thinking of someone and then bumping into them randomly confirm your deep connection with soul and consciousness.

The teachings of Guatama Buddha reinforce self-respect, understanding and accountability to reduce pain and human sufferance. Being conscious of your own actions is essential if you wish to grow into a higher state of being. True growth is initiated when you don't hide but confront your own opinions however misguided and uncomfortable they are.

Cosmic Master Guatama Buddha reminds you to respect yourself and others; you must remember that respect is earned from the actions you take. Rise above the victim consciousness. Self-love, compassion and understanding will assist in personal realisations while you seek respect from your family, employment and social groups.

Following in the footsteps of the earth's cosmic master and taking a path to a higher level of enlightened consciousness is time consuming. We are all born and raised with certain prejudices, so it is up to us as individuals to change these prejudices the more we become aware of them. If you are triggered emotionally, take the path of a higher understanding.

'Make the most of your situation. There is always a lesson of truth to seek.'

– *GUATAMA BUDDHA*

Sacred crystal: golden topaz

Affirmation: *'I am open to new experiences. I realise my purpose with passion.'*

8 Cosmic gateway

Insecurities. Connection with others. Refocusing.

8 Cosmic gateway

Insecurities. Connection with others. Refocusing.

The cosmic gateway, a portal that connects souls to the universal multiverse, is accessible via trance states and meditation through our central light column, opening the cosmic gateway to the soul's sacred light. Like a flower, nurturing and care of its environment allows the soul to bloom in its own precious time.

The path to self-realisation is filled with conscious awakenings. Our mind is a powerful tool that when fully open and activated can connect our being to light sources unimaginable to the naked eye. When the sacred light of the cosmic gateway shines upon the world, the individual acceleration of self-awareness through self-realisation can reveal the body's capability of healing itself.

Ascension Master Yogananda announces that you are in a time of great personal change and growth. Don't be afraid to start over again or of finding fresh ways to support the life you want with joy and happiness. If you feel overwhelmed, reduce excessive workloads as you work through this process.

Yogananda suggests practising self-realisation as you work through any feelings of sadness or melancholy you have about the past or what you are seeking to change. Challenge yourself to try new things or join a self-help group that aligns with your global or personal interests.

'Balance will restore when the mind is restored.'

– ASCENSION MASTER YOGANANDA

Sacred crystal: rhodonite

Affirmation: *'I am my own master. I hold the answers within me. My energy is limitless.'*

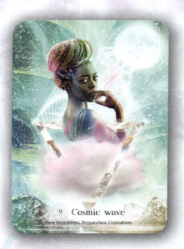

9 Cosmic wave

New friendships. Preparation. Custodians.

9 Cosmic wave

New friendships. Preparation. Custodians.

Spiritually, cosmic waves symbolise the divine illumination of energetic vibration. Light is fractal, with different wavelengths aligning to the energy centres of the body and levels of ascension. The resonance of the cosmic waves permeates our divine self for greater illumination and healing accessing our divine blueprint, DNA and cellular memory in an instant.

Embodying the presence of divine wisdom, enlightenment and magical connection, the earth's ascension keeper

Kuthumi oversees this cosmic transference through the earth's sacred light keepers and ascension masters, who are charged with the caretaking of souls on earth. The northern and southern lights beautify their magnificence.

Ascension Master Kuthumi requests that you clear your mind, opening your presence to accept the wisdom of the earth's light keepers. This cosmic wave of pure intelligence is yours to access but you must examine your energetic receptivity. As your intelligent mind and emotional body begin to accept these new light frequencies and the wisdom of the keepers, your energy will align to the divine sequence.

Kuthumi asks you to prepare your physical body so you may receive divine messages in all their beautiful glory. Connecting to the cosmic wave through bright colours such as pink, green and blue will amplify your intuitive presence and cosmic connection, awakening memories of the past and distant lifetimes for greater healing and accelerated learning for the earth and humanity.

'The world is at your feet. Explore the earth around you with new appreciation.'

– KUTHUMI

Sacred crystal: Herkimer diamond

Affirmation: *'My frequency rises in perfect resonance. I accept this integration with love.'*

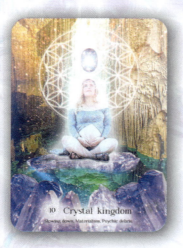

10 Crystal kingdom
Slowing down. Materialism. Psychic debris.

10 Crystal kingdom

Slowing down. Materialism. Psychic debris.

Our earth mother is in a constant state of creation. Crystalline structures are found all over the planet from small pockets in bedrock to underground cave systems that once entered seem like an endless fortress. Their growth is a constant evolution, continually servicing the planet with their transmuting and energetic presence.

Volcanic eruptions create the environmental cleanser and purification stone black obsidian, which easily clears negativity. It is only fitting that mother earth produces her own environmental cleanser on such a grand scale, demanding respect during this process.

Earth mother Gaia is never in a rush to complete a process. There is always an earthly system that is followed in a divine order to achieve an earthly cycle and equilibrium. Without the interruption of man, Gaia's beauty can be witnessed through pristine waters as nature thrives in harmonic balance. But like the volcano ready to erupt with molten hot lava, emotions are bubbling to the surface.

Strong and resilient, Ascended Master Gaia recognises the lack of personal harmony. Rushing to complete plans or becoming anxious or impatient that your dreams or visions aren't happening fast enough will only force errors or mistakes as you try to achieve them. Just like the crystal growing and forming beneath the surface with divine plan, you must devise your own plan and move forward with action.

'Release the expectation of perfection. A flower will still bloom in a balanced environment.'

– ASCENDED MASTER GAIA

Sacred crystal: tanzanite

Affirmation: *'I choose my words with careful consideration. I speak with kindness.'*

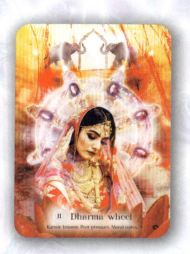

11 Dharma wheel

Karmic lessons. Peer pressure. Moral codes.

In today's age it is impossible to go through life without having your moral code and ethics challenged by people and society. In the past, peer pressure, discrimination, racism and social discourse taught you to be suspicious of the motives and actions of others. The realisation of knowing right from wrong, in any context, is what your soul is seeking now during its experience: the law of truth.

When the dharma wheel spins you will be provided with pathways that lead to personal truths. Finding yourself in compromising situations with questionable people or intentions will only add more weight to your dharma scale. Lies and secrets will be revealed now. Honour your agreements. Be wary of unsolicited advice and of those that wish to gossip about others.

Seated on the sacred lotus, Ascension Master Lady Lakshmi questions your morality and ethics. Challenges to your integrity are revealed, with a risk of theft and deceit, personal robbery and damage to personal or business interests. Be aware of your surroundings and social environments and of suspicious activities.

Dressed in red and surrounded by white elephants, Lady Lakshmi influences luck in business and prosperity. Reduce your exposure to negative social settings by keeping your distance, even if only short term, from new and unfamiliar people including volatile atmospheres and high-energy events. Balance your dharma by seeking your personal truth without compromising your integrity or morality.

'Let the wrap of cloth untwine. Let thought flow with breath.'

– ASCENSION MASTER LADY LAKSHMI

Sacred crystal: garnet

Affirmation: *'I control my thoughts and feelings. I act with integrity and grace.'*

12 Divine creation

Acceptance. Personal commitments. Euphoria

12 Divine creation

Acceptance. Personal commitments. Euphoria.

Divine creation is boundless; it can transform your life into one of peace and joy. Having the awareness and experience of divine creation encourages you to love deeper, have more compassion, understand troubled souls and nurture all living creatures with a loving abundance. Uncontrolled by religion or dogma, divine love is always accessible; you only need to open your heart and mind to receive its creative presence.

The life of divine creation is free flowing and endless. Knowing that you are worthy of accepting this divinity enhances your personal power with creative force. Divine creation is divine love, and although the soul grasps this love openly the physical body cannot contain it.

Divine love is intense and overwhelming, often leaving a person momentarily euphoric when cultivated with a divine awakening.

Under the wings of the Ascension Master Goddess Isis, her aura can resurrect your spirit into a life filled with more love as she assists you to release guilt surrounding self-acceptance and family matters. The magic of her presence is automatically uplifting, protecting those that seek her wisdom and guidance.

Ascension Master Goddess Isis asks that you release your feelings of guilt, mistrust, vulnerability and betrayal. Old relationship wounds, abuse and the violation of personal rights have stopped you from embracing yourself fully. Understanding your personal needs on such an intimate level requires a self-loving attitude. Re-evaluate your circumstances after professional assistance.

'Making magic is an act of divine love.
Divine love is divine creation.'

– *ASCENSION MASTER ISIS*

Sacred crystal: emerald

Affirmation: *'I am safe sharing my vulnerability with others.'*

13 Energy attachments

Energy exchange. Negative influences. Self-sabotage.

13 Energy attachments

Energy exchange. Negative influences. Self-sabotage.

You are a conscious creator; how you address the energy in
your life determines how it is directed around you. Emotional
energy, spiritual entities and negative energy frequencies have
the potential to disrupt your life force, misdirecting your
thoughts towards lower vibrational actions such as addictions,
mental and emotional instability and other non-loving
pathways filled with self-sabotage and critical judgement.

Forever in a deep state of awareness and tranquillity, Lord
Shiva is held as a supreme being and is depicted in two poses:

meditation and dance. The divine masculine is carried by Lord Shiva as his power and presence encompass a love of all life, choosing to protect those who cannot protect themselves. Known for rescuing other gods and spiritual beings by agreeing to swallow the blue poison halāhala, he was able to save all living beings and bring order to the world.

Any state of fear will weaken your auric fields, making it more challenging to keep attachments away and to keep control of your energy. Lord Shiva asks you to address any parasitic connections or energy attachments that have been draining your vitality, influencing and interrupting thought processes.

Ascension Master Lord Shiva holds the power of destruction and creation within his grasp, suggesting that you regain control over your own energy exchanges and remove energetic ties that are consuming your life in a negative way, reducing spiritual manipulation. Dance and body movement will lighten your heart to let go and free yourself from old restrictions.

> 'Holding on to anger is swallowing poison.
> Be at peace with your demons.'
>
> – ASCENSION MASTER LORD SHIVA

Sacred crystal: shungite

Affirmation: *'I remove imbalanced energy with ease. I am secure. I am safe.'*

14 Energy medicine
Sensuality. Devotion. Celestial fertility. Deep rest.

14 Energy medicine

Sensuality. Devotion. Celestial fertility. Deep rest.

Energy medicine is often used to describe healing actions of light-based energy, the direction of flow of kundalini and the interaction of living light energy with the human body. All forms of energy medicine, including homeopathic, reiki, tantra and yoga, fall under methods of spiritual and energetic practice.

Unbound by time and space, energy medicine can address any issue from any time in your life that requires balanced intervention. A transitive sound bath of song that resonates with your current state of being integrates any energetic practice you choose to implement on your mind, body and soul.

The golden Ascension Goddess Master Paravati asks that you relax and fall into your creative and sensual self, which was born from the sacred fire. Deep rest can be found when you surrender your energy to mountainous places, the birthplace of Paravati. Her divine energy medicine can adjust any imperfect vibrations surrounding sensuality, your home life and feminine imbalance combined with your conscious action.

Paravati's divine strength and power is clearly demonstrated as her golden resonance flows between all connections of life in balanced power. This divine manifestation of the divine feminine brings fertile energy that will nurture any seeds you have planted. Celestial sounds combined with divine devotion will produce fertile gardens for you to plant seeds for any outcome your heart desires. Give them time to grow with positive energy medicine.

'You are a living being of divine expression.
Radiate your magnificence.'

– *ASCENDED MASTER PARAVATI*

Sacred crystal: creedite

Affirmation: *'I share my sacred self with divine love. I resonate in harmony.'*

15 Galactic vibration

Personal conviction.
Raising your resilience. Direct channel.

15 Galactic vibration

Personal conviction.
Raising your resilience. Direct channel.

'Ohm' was thought to be the first sound heard throughout the universe. The mystical syllable has been associated with cosmic sound and divine principles for centuries. While scientists can only speculate at the age of the universe, its vibrational influence continues to alter the earth's surface and structure.

A galactic connection often feels like a lightning bolt, shooting down through your higher crown at the speed of light. Being energetically tapped by a higher, dimensional galactic energy of evolved consciousness is an intense experience and not one to be taken lightly. These high energies of 100 per cent pure light consciousness operate on a vastly different scale to any other energy form. Those that experience these connections are direct channellers; caution is *always* required at this level.

The galactic vibration is one of divine expression. The universe's continual energy expansion alongside the remnants of its early beginnings is the very reality of creative and divine intelligence. Galactic Ascension Master Galadriel is encouraging you to explore your innate connection to the universal god spark. As you are called to a higher purpose you will be a support and strength for others who experience troubled times.

Continuing in the face of your own adversity builds resilience and conviction of spirit. The photographic beauty of star systems will inspire you to further your connection to the stars as you gaze at the wonder of their mysterious, universal creation, reminding you to aim high and reach for the stars.

> *'Helping humanity is also a conscious choice to help yourself.'*
>
> *– GALACTIC MASTER GALADRIEL*

Sacred crystal: tektite

Affirmation: *'I activate my galactic vibration for higher humanity. I speak with informed guidance.'*

16 Golden light ray

Love and laughter. Receiving and giving gifts.
Passionate projects.

16 Golden light ray

**Love and laughter. Receiving and giving gifts.
Passionate projects.**

The golden ray is on the 12th ray of creation, the highest frequency and also known as Christ consciousness. It is a high-frequency healing channel that connects to the central sun. The golden ray can gently awaken your kundalini and accelerate your spiritual growth the more you choose to work with its vibration.

The golden light ray anchors creator energy into the remaining light rays throughout the universe and earth, creating and influencing planetary healing and releasing energetic denseness as its wavelengths move across the multiverse. The ray can initiate soul awakenings that bring your perception of all that is into closer mental focus.

Floating along the golden ray, Ascension Master Lord Maitreya disrupts dense and melancholic emotions. He encourages you to see the lighter side of life so that laughter and comedic relief can benefit you. Use colour therapy; pause and take a breath. Laughter is medicine for the soul.

Generosity and abundance follow the golden ray wherever it leads. It is pure divinity that seeks to heal those who access its frequency. Much like the setting sun, its colour is warm and luminous, settling our soul when we feel its glow. Always uplifting, the golden ray will shower you with the warmth and comfort of fulfilment as it settles the highs and lows of emotions, shifting feelings of loss and emptiness within the psyche of your soul.

'Find joy in laughing at yourself more often.'

– ASCENSION MASTER LORD MAITREYA

Sacred crystal: opal

Affirmation: *'I am golden, I am radiant, I am abundant. I accept these gifts with an open heart.'*

17 Inner oracle

You are the channel. Déjà vu. Self-fulfilling prophecy.

Receiving the knowledge and wisdom that is offered from deep illumination can often be prophetic and life affirming, and will help you to know you are on the right path. Powerful realisations, prophetic vision, past-life memories and soul connections are triggered by the oracle that is centred deep within you.

The wisdom of the inner oracle is often buried within. Discovering its presence illuminates past mistakes, bad choices and ego-based relationships with yourself and others.

Revealing this connection can trigger internal defences, making it difficult to maintain a solid connection to the intelligence of your oracle.

Dedicated to illuminate the earth, Lord Lanto asks you to learn and grow your inner oracle with discussion, seeing the world with eyes of wisdom and acknowledging that you are still a student learning in the great cycle of life. Accepting possible errors in judgements allows your consciousness to adapt, redirecting energy to a new outcome.

Holding the flame of illumination on the Second Ray, Ascension Master Lord Lanto encourages you to become closer to your sense of knowing. Explore your psychic self and intuition as you examine previous signs and events where déjà vu has been experienced. Sudden realisations will occur now; having the courage to openly accept them is what initiates the act of enlightenment.

'Mastery is the key to self success.
Discipline your mind.'

– *ASCENSION MASTER LORD LANTO*

Sacred crystal: labradorite

Affirmation: *'I am constantly learning. I illuminate my presence with each lesson.'*

18 Language of light
Rediscovery. Humble wanderer. Communication.

18 Language of light

Rediscovery. Humble wanderer. Communication.

The language of light is written among sound waves and
frequencies. Any object that has a high resonance falls
within the light language and is multidimensional. Often
when viewing the language of light, symbols, numbers
and geometry take centre stage. One example of this
language resides within the realm of sacred geometry and
is often used in energy clearing, sacred intentions, prayer,
meditation and mindful practice.

Water spirits such as dolphins, whales and seahorses have unique alignments with light languages. These graceful water creatures emit high-frequency sound waves that shatter dense energy fields with precision and purpose. Highly intelligent and protective, these beautiful beings will share their mystical intelligence if you meet them with respect, humility and peace.

Galactic guides the Seven Sisters request you immerse yourself in higher frequencies that can uplift your soul and spirit to improve your vitality. Rediscover the old and ancient, reduce waste and upcycle to help the environment: this simplicity will make room for new energy, bringing more joy to your life.

The communication of light language through your celestial channel will encourage you to try new things, including interest in travelling to foreign lands and learning new languages that support your personal and spiritual growth. Just as with learning a new language, try not to get lost in spirit translation.

*'Serenity comes with peaceful
actions. Speak with silence.'*

– COSMIC ASCENSION GUIDES THE SEVEN SISTERS

Sacred crystal: larimar

Affirmation: *'I hear the language of light clearly. I speak with renewed spirit.'*

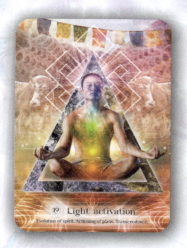

19 Light activation

Evolution of spirit. Actioning of plans. Transcendence.

19 Light activation

Evolution of spirit. Actioning of plans. Transcendence.

When the body lights up in an attunement or activation it triggers a beacon for the soul to communicate with the physical body. Overseen by the ancient Tibetan master Djwhal Khul, activations can bring deep healing and transcendence. Regardless of physical sensation, these activations occur on an energetic and emotional level.

Activations, which can be physical or spiritual in nature, amplify your personal connections with the world and energy around you. Essential for the evolution of human consciousness, activating energy centres, intuition, healing abilities, life force or kundalini can happen gently or abruptly given your chosen personal path.

Awakening dormant DNA and hidden memories, activations are dominantly positive experiences that encourage your mind to connect more closely to your soul and spirit. Transmissions, awakenings and spiritual prophecy will occur now so have a paper and pen ready.

Ascension Master Djwhal Khul asks you to be clear with your intentions, as conflicts will be triggered by stress. Choose to let go of fear and let your soul guide you on a journey of self-discovery. Your soul is in a constant state of learning, so learning a new skill and planning future education are favourable now. Be realistic in your approach otherwise you will set yourself up to fail, repeating self-sabotaging behaviours. Being stubborn will only keep you stuck in places that your soul doesn't want to be in.

*'Your soul is seeking new challenges.
Let yourself be free.'*

– *ASCENDED MASTER DJWHAL KHUL*

Sacred crystal: charoite

Affirmation: *'I activate and awaken
my soul's divine intelligence.'*

20 Light body
Independence brings comfort.
Past restrictions. Ancestral healing.

20 Light body

Independence brings comfort.
Past restrictions. Ancestral healing.

Every human being has a light body, a vessel for our consciousness as it instantaneously transfers the knowledge of past, present, DNA coding and galactic memory. It is a sacred grid interwoven with sacred geometry encapsulating your physical, emotional, mental and spiritual being. For those who are beginning the spiritual journey your light body is just beginning to shine.

Once this light infusion takes place within the light body your soul's matrix begins to settle, and you will find a fresh sense of balance. This new alignment brings positive experiences as this light awakening transmutes denser karmic debris and patterns that have kept you stuck and stagnant in the past.

Ascended Master Lady Portia asks you to act independently, as low self-confidence and self-esteem can improve with independent action. Reliance on co-dependent relationships will leave you unbalanced and insecure about your life. Learn to rely on yourself above all others.

Resonating on the Seventh Ray, Lady Portia's divine action helps to release and heal trapped ancestral karma. You must be ready to shed the old shell that has provided you with so much protection and comfort. While you may feel unbalanced or unprepared, you are ready to end generational patterns and cycles now.

'Trade your shield for an arrow.'

– *ASCENSION MASTER LADY PORTIA*

Sacred crystal: aquamarine

Affirmation: *'I infuse my light body with power and presence. I embrace my divinity.'*

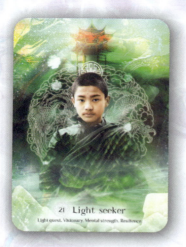

21 Light seeker

Light quest. Visionary. Mental strength. Resilience.

21 Light seeker

Light quest. Visionary. Mental strength. Resilience.

We are all born as light bringers but not all choose to follow the path of a light seeker, someone who is not afraid to confront controversial issues head on for they know that to find a way to the light is to hold a torch through the darkness. Always searching for truth, enlightenment and connection to the divine, it is a blessing to share and gift the power of light, love and illumination to all those you meet.

Built over stages and many failures, the light seeker builds their resilience through understanding and compassion.

Their quest for the light of the divine brings them to a path of constant learning, educating themselves about the true nature and calling of their soul. They see through the matrix that confuses and disorientates those whose souls remain unawakened, trapped in cycles of ego, fear, self-fulfilment and control-based paradigms.

Ascended Master Confucius suggests you build skills of the mind. When freed of mental limitations, human action becomes innovative, powerful and fearless. Confucious breaks down any complexity simply so you can adapt or make small changes to areas that are being challenged.

You will be drawn to light-orientated actions. Align your mind with how you present yourself. This higher calling, or light quest, will bring you closer to your divine light. As your light begins to shine brighter than ever, the path you walk will become clearer and more in focus. As Confucious reminds us all, when the student is ready the teacher will appear.

'What is time, when there is only present action?'

– ASCENDED MASTER CONFUCIOUS

Sacred crystal: jade

Affirmation: *'I control my view of success. My achievements speak for themselves.'*

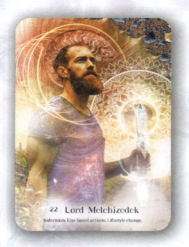

22 Lord Melchizedek

Indecision. Ego-based actions. Lifestyle change.

22 Lord Melchizedek

Indecision. Ego-based actions. Lifestyle change.

Lord Melchizedek is a true leader of the spiritual hierarchy. A multidimensional being and Lord of the First Ray, he is a teacher for those who choose to free themselves from the bonds of ego to reach a higher state of being. Observing your path with great interest, he will assist you to know your soul more closely and help you connect to your own divine cosmic presence.

Allying with Lord Melchizedek is an intense experience; not everyone is spiritually and emotionally ready to create this connection. Your crown and third eye chakras receive intense downloads of energy that often needs rest for integration. This higher source of knowledge is only accessible by making clear choices to remove ego-based patterns and choices.

Standing with his rod of power, Ascension Guide Lord Melchizedek asks that you be clear with your decisions. You must learn to assert your authority by embracing your autonomy. Just like a stern father figure, you must stand up for yourself and refuse to let people push you around.

It is time to do things differently. Allow Lord Melchizedek to illuminate personal ignorance and ego so you can make clear choices that support your lifestyle. Being clear with what you expect from yourself and others will negate any anguish or anxiety you have about connecting to the sacred light of your soul. Embrace your inner spark.

'Become what it is you seek.
Stand alone if you must.'

– *ASCENDED MASTER LORD MELCHIZEDEK*

Sacred crystal: clear quartz

Affirmation: *'I respect the authority I am given. My choices bring respect and achievement.'*

23 Magical alchemy
Innovation. Ingenuity. Curiosity. Ahead of your time.

23 Magical alchemy

Innovation. Ingenuity. Curiosity. Ahead of your time.

Alchemy has always been viewed as a magical process. Ancient alchemic practice was usually performed in secrecy from fear of persecution and possible death, as the misunderstanding of chemistry in pre-mediaeval times meant it was often associated with demonic practice and with witchcraft and sacred magic.

The magician Merlin is the ultimate alchemist, as he cohesively combined medicinal power and scientific principles to better the lives of himself and others through alchemic practice. Ingenious and resourceful, the developments created by his humbled curiosity have inspired generations.

Ascended Guide Merlin is here to place you on purpose. While you may feel your ideas are ahead of your time, brainstorming needs to be actioned. Strong opinions or fascinations with the world of alchemy, witchcraft and magic encourage you to explore the enchantment of manifestation and creative invention. It's time to make and create, to get your hands dirty!

Explore creative impulses. Design and innovate. Let go of what you think you cannot do. When you place your mind on purpose, magic happens. Take advantage and illustrate your endeavours and future goals while Merlin's energy is at its peak.

'Mysteries are unsolved problems. Problems are challenges that need to be faced.'

– ASCENDED MASTER MERLIN

Sacred crystal: merlinite

Affirmation: *'I acknowledge my inner magic. It is guided with loving creation.'*

24 Past life

A cultural experience. It is behind you. Regression.

24 Past life

A cultural experience. It is behind you. Regression.

Reincarnation is a belief held by many different religions and cultures. Deep attractions to foreign cultural items such as clothing, animals and architecture are just some connections to your past-life memories. Obsessions with and passion about events, tools, professions or objects is your soul reminding you of previous experiences that have taught you valuable lessons.

While past-life regression can be extremely beneficial in understanding your interactions with family, friends and purpose, understanding these traumas can help identify the reasoning behind debilitating psychological conditions such as phobias and fears in your current life. Obsessing over past events and experiences highlights the soul's need to achieve equilibrium in the present.

Cosmic Master Lord Krishna calls your mind to address the past, bringing healing and closure to unanswered chapters of your life. These unexplained and sometimes irrational emotions represent the challenges destined to enlighten the soul on its divine path. Be present.

Serving on the Second Ray, Lord Krishna asks you to heal and address past-life memories and karmic issues now. Questioning authority and fear of failure will highlight these fears so you can free the chains of the past. Meditate. Avoid being mentally stuck in the past, as the time is now. Affirm your soul's desires to the sacred breath of the universe.

'Internal desires lead to temptations. Send your prayers through the cosmos.'

– MASTER LORD KRISHNA

Sacred crystal: Shiva lingam

Affirmation: *'I am grounded in the present. My heart is centred and focused on today.'*

25 Power of presence

A power struggle. Unlock your potential. Authenticity.

25 Power of presence

A power struggle. Unlock your potential. Authenticity.

To have the power of presence is to hold your heart's confidence in all areas of your life. Those who have the power of presence are often charming and inspiring, commanding the attention of others. To have influential presence you must be a great communicator, taking humble pride in your life's achievements and expressing yourself authentically.

However, people with presence have the potential to manipulate others who are unsure of their own persona. Cult leaders have mastered their personal presence to influence others for negative reasons. Having a strong presence can create egotistical attitudes. Be cautious of self-proclaimed businesspeople, gurus and those who seek fame and fortune.

The powerful earth Ascension Master Chief Sitting Bull identifies your need to create strong boundaries and personal presence. The eagle feathers in his beautiful headdress represent the ancient wisdom between the land and human spirit carried by the light of his soul. He asks you to stand tall and speak from your heart. Words are powerful, but your actions speak louder.

Connect to Chief Sitting Bull when you need to enforce a strong mental attitude. You are a catalyst that uplifts and changes those you meet along the way, although you may appear arrogant and materialistic. Stay humble and true to gratuitous principles. You are divinely designed to empower others with your passion.

> *'Sinful actions come from greedy*
> *souls. Harm none.'*
>
> – *ASCENSION MASTER CHIEF SITTING BULL*

Sacred crystal: turquoise

Affirmation: *'I am a powerful presence. I am humble and gracious when communicating with others.'*

26 Sacred space

**Positive outcome. Clarity.
Lucky attraction. Removing obstacles.**

Regardless of philosophy or religion, all individuals have a sacred space they retreat to when needing solace, prayer or reflection to heal the mind, body and spirit. Sacred spaces are often religious centres such as cathedrals, monasteries and churches but can also be rainforest waterfalls or tranquil ponds. Unbound by location, it only needs to be an area that you find comfort in when connecting to your spiritual self.

Setting a sacred space is essential to create a focused spiritual sanctuary, as you are setting a tone and vibration for that area to amplify your personal power and universal energy. While you may find you have no time for routine or imperfections, regular space clearing will keep your vibration high and your mind clear.

Cosmic Master Lord Ganesha offers seekers the knowledge of sacred purity from the Fifth Ray. Let more light in to brighten your space to cleanse your energy fields. Using traditional herbs and offerings, this cosmic master will release trapped and murky energy, transmuting energetic portals that have interfered with the natural balance and positive feng shui.

The elephant master can clear obstacles that are interfering with your life. Ascension Master Lord Ganesha requests you find your sacred space. By carefully cutting away old energy to connect you to a clearer path, Lord Ganesha can bring you closer to divine manifestation, your desires and personal dharma.

*'Sacred ceremonies will bring
rewarding resolutions.'*

– ASCENSION MASTER LORD GANESHA

Sacred crystal: tourmalinated quartz

Affirmation: *'I am clear. I am cleansed.
My soul is whole and complete.'*

27 Scales of karma

Cycle of disharmony. Creating new traditions.
Unfortunate events.

27 Scales of karma

**Cycle of disharmony. Creating new traditions.
Unfortunate events.**

Life can often become a balancing act: juggling your physical needs with the needs of those around you, including family, can sometimes challenge your love light. Giving without the expectation of receiving is one way of achieving a better state of karma. You must look to find positive experiences from harsh lessons.

When people feel good they do good. When feeling down people are more likely to throw emotional and energetic daggers towards those who have hurt them, even if it's only temporary. You must be self-aware as your emotional reactivity will dictate the balance of the energetic scale. Any negativity or toxicity can be purged now if you are willing to open your heart space and detach from these cycles.

The benevolent Ascended Master Maha Chohan seeks your understanding. Teaching light seekers of the spiritual and angelic hierarchy, his learnings encourage the soul to balance and correct its journey back to the sacred heart. His white head scarf reminds seekers to create more positive and loving interactions with purity, to keep your scales better balanced.

The blessed Maha Chohan asks you to be aware of your conscious thought of others. Speaking negatively about a person only continues to further a cycle of negativity. Snap out of it! Acting in the heat of the moment will leave you red faced and embarrassed. Examine the brightness of your love light. Protect your heart but keep it open.

> *'Sit with the unfortunate, for they will see you as I see you.'*
> – *ASCENDED MASTER MAHA CHOHAN*

Sacred crystal: amethyst

Affirmation: *'I relinquish control over expectation. I am free.'*

28 Soul family

Happy reunions. Support. Order from chaos.

28 Soul family

Happy reunions. Support. Order from chaos.

Your soul family consists of people who empower you to be
your best self. Their wisdom and experience give your soul
a comfortable space to share your joy or heartache. These
members inspire and nurture, gently guiding you to your
purpose in this lifetime; feeling completely understood
without saying a word is one of their key attributes.

Meeting someone in your soul family is like finding a
needle in a haystack: they are not easy to find and difficult
to spot if you don't know what you are looking for. When

you meet them your heart and higher heart chakra make an instantaneous connection. Mutual unconditional and divine love is shared in an instant as soul connections are remembered at the deepest level.

Ascended Master Osiris supports you in reconnecting with old friends or family members. Happy reunions bring wisdom and understanding as you free yourself of burdens and insecurities. Reconnections will be made now that initiate new friendships, bringing closure to memories of the past. Often appearing as the great shepherd, he sees the flock before him and knows when to communicate or intervene directly.

Much like Osiris, restoration and life surrounding family will bring order and disorder. Spend time with chosen family through celebrations or casual get togethers, reliving stories of love, laughter and the lessons in between. Reconnect to your soul family, for they are your best teachers.

'Make your love attainable. No one can receive what you cannot give.'

– ASCENDED MASTER OSIRIS

Sacred crystal: malachite

Affirmation: *'I am confident to stand alone. I am all I need.'*

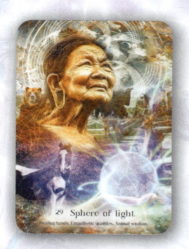

29 Sphere of light

Healing hands. Empathetic qualities. Animal wisdom.

29 Sphere of light

Healing hands. Empathetic qualities. Animal wisdom.

Not to be confused with angel or spiritual orbs, the sphere of light is pure light consciousness. It is translucent, bright, energetic shimmering light that can grow to any size with conscious thought and psychic energy. This intelligence is designed to grow and adapt through conscious thought and action.

Secondary spheres of light, also known as psychic energy balls, can be created through the hand chakras to utilise healing energy or manifesting, assisting you through a specific struggle or obstacle. They can be directed to anyone and anything with different intents.

Ascended Master White Buffalo Calf Woman asks you to focus on commitment and conservation. Be empathetically mindful of the energy you are sending out into the universe, as difficult people can trigger your emotions. Activate your healing hands when challenged empathically to help yourself and others. Respecting the earth and all of its people requires conscious observation with positive action for change.

White Buffalo Calf Woman wishes for you to understand your personal connection to the earth and preserve all living animals. She asks you to be consistent with your actions and extend your light to all living creatures, to learn more about their divine connection and importance to spirit through the ages.

'Respect the way of our animal teachers.
Listen to their messages.'

~ ASCENSION MASTER WHITE BUFFALO CALF WOMAN

Sacred crystal: azurite

Affirmation: *'I clear and activate*
my healing hands to assist my soul
in healing myself and others.'

30 Spirit guides
Looking for signs. Philosophical discussion. Supervision.

30 Spirit guides

Looking for signs. Philosophical discussion. Supervision.

Before your earthly birth your soul discusses with the spiritual hierarchy your soul's path, karmic lessons, specific details and other souls you would like to write into your human story. Once you have passed this plan to the hierarchy it is approved and sealed for your earthly descension. It is here that your soul's spiritual guides are chosen to guide you through life.

A spiritual guide is assigned at birth, and as you grow new guides step forward to assist you in specific tasks, transformations, passions and awakenings. From animals to angelic guides, ascended masters to religious figures, you will be made aware of these deep connections through synchronicities, signs, vision quests and serendipity moments.

The father of Taoism, Master Lao Tzu, instructs that in order to become who you desire to be your intelligent mind must expand to reach a stage of personal and spiritual freedom. Reduce argumentative discussion and increase inclusivity by philosophical action. Change is growth, an inevitable task of life that often feels uncomfortable.

Ancient Ascension Master Lao Tzu brings surprises and changing plans, asking you to listen more and speak less but with deeper meaning. Disconnect from excessive drama. A new guide steps forward now to supervise your earthly quest for soul experience. To be open to these experiences, silence your mind and connect through meditative practice.

'Make peace with the past. Overcome the fear within you. Calmness is key.'

– ASCENSION MASTER LAO TZU

Sacred crystal: brookite

Affirmation: *'I activate the sacred power within me. It rises clearly and gently.'*

31 Temple of Mary

Emotional expression. Playful innocence. Exploitation.

31 Temple of Mary

Emotional expression. Playful innocence. Exploitation.

An organ of deep knowledge and wisdom, your heart links your consciousness and soul as one being. Receiving this divine love can be an intense and heart-awakening experience. This divine expansion communicates these interactions via your heart's feeling its emotional expression is essential to give and receive love fully.

The Temple of Mary is guarded fiercely. Those that choose to enter must be ready to free their heart from love restrictions. With humility and grace, the divine mother can help you identify any wounds connected to mother figures with loving support. She inspires your soul to love deeper and surrender to the innocence of your inner child.

Residing on the Fifth Ray of healing, the divine Mother Mary assists the children of earth to evolve their heart to free individuals from emotional pain and burden. If unconditional love wasn't given to you as a child it may be difficult to accept who you are and others without conditions. Left unhealed, these wounds affect future relationships and acceptance of love, leaving your generous heart open to exploitation.

Divine Mother Mary asks you to be receptive in expanding into new levels of love. Get the tissues ready! Goodbyes will seem to last forever, and empathetic connections will bring newfound friends. Long distance travel, relationship issues and natural life transitions will also influence friendships and relationships.

'Your heart is heavy. Love and be loved. Be at peace, child.'

– *ASCENSION MASTER DIVINE MOTHER MARY*

Sacred crystal: morganite

Affirmation: *'I release my personal prejudice. I accept others the way I accept myself.'*

32 Temple secrets

Secrecy. Isolation. Observation. Ritual magic.

32 Temple secrets

Secrecy. Isolation. Observation. Ritual magic.

With sacred ritual and practical magic, a temple holds many secrets about its people and purpose and its ancient traditional practice. Temples are sacred spaces that can reveal hidden mysteries about the soul and psyche. When you connect to the divine through temple magic, secrets of the universe can be unlocked and witnessed.

The alchemic practice of sacred ritual can be observed through deep chants, devout prayer and the vows held sacred within the walls of each temple. The secrets held in temple ritual must be honoured by the seeker and keepers of the temple's divine and hidden magic. Their sacred light beckons each seeker, igniting past-life recall on their spiritual quest.

Residing on the green ray, Ascension Master Hilarion asks you to seek and hear truth with open ears. Your spoken word reflects your integrity, so be direct and assertive. Combine your creative and analytical mind to find answers buried in your soul's intelligence. A master of science, Hilarion asks you to connect further to your inner light through discovery using a methodical, systematic approach to your goals and life quest.

Connect further to your inner light through discovery and method, and honour your inner temple with a devout practice. Not everyone sees the world as you do; ask Hilarion to bring the light of illumination to unveil the path of self-discovery. Be careful of tempting offers from other people, as they come with hidden catches.

'The cycle of justice returns. The cycle continues with a lesson learned.'

– *ASCENSION MASTER HILARION*

Sacred crystal: aurichalcite

Affirmation: *'I awaken the truth within me. I hear my soul's message clearly.'*

33 Tibetan fire serpent

Seeking a higher truth. Discernment.
A better path. Authority.

33 Tibetan fire serpent

**Seeking a higher truth. Discernment.
A better path. Authority.**

Snakes have always been viewed as sacred medicinal creatures. The very shedding of their skin is connected to transformation, healing and immortal life. The Tibetan fire serpent heals the spiritual state of its recipient; its energy flows in an upward spiral with intense power and magnification.

When the fire serpent rises its energy unlocks, releasing blocked and stagnant energy as it ascends from the base chakra. By transmuting energy, it cleanses the spirit on a cellular level. A master of the First Ray, El Morya assists with grounding this sacred energy into the lower chakras and opening those towards the crown to create balance and harmony within the physical, mental and spiritual bodies.

Ascended Master El Morya chooses to share the wisdom of the ancients with those who seek a higher truth. Emphasising self-mastery, El Morya suggests you unclutter your life with authority and discernment. Fire up! Determination and perseverance will help shake up rigid ideas and open experiences so you are living life at its fullest. You were born to thrive, not just survive.

Visit your sacred space to activate the sleeping serpent, and ground your heart and anchor your spiritual self. Your needs have changed over time and so should your daily practice. Be brutally honest with yourself. Life is about showing up; be there and be present. You are never too small to make a difference.

'You are the centre of your universe.
Is your sun shining?'

– ASCENDED MASTER EL MORYA

Sacred crystal: blue kyanite

Affirmation: *'I release old energy with love and gratitude. I am free to explore my heart's desire.'*

34 Universal Merkabah

A sacred purpose. You have the answer.
Lucid dreaming.

34 Universal Merkabah

**A sacred purpose. You have the answer.
Lucid dreaming.**

The universal Merkabah awakens a deeper experience of the human consciousness. The personal Merkabah that surrounds your aura connects you to the universal Merkabah matrix paradigm with a fine platinum thread. This allows you to astral travel and access different levels of consciousness.

Connected to the unified mind, the universal Merkabah enhances your perception of self-awareness and communication with the emotional or feeling body. Talking to the self in this way improves intuitive sensitivity, inner knowing and the ability to sense and understand emotional imbalances when bodily pain and sensations occur.

Often viewed as being seated on a great white throne, Ascension Master Sanat Kumara asks you to recall your life experiences. Connect to your inner guru for wisdom and purpose. While learning can be difficult, it is essential you save yourself from personal destruction. Visionary and lucid dreaming experiences will reinforce your intuitive senses and unique connection to the ascension and astral realms.

The wise master asks you to set yourself free and deny any influence that is not 100 per cent pure light source. Calling you closer to your soul's sacred light, the unified mind resets your universal Merkabah to resonate in harmonic perfection with Sanat Kumara's guidance. When your Merkabah is aligned, be prepared to say goodbye to those who wish to take advantage and keep you stuck in the status quo.

'The power of love unifies all. You are love. Love your temple.'

– *ASCENDED MASTER LORD SANAT KUMARA*

Sacred crystal: benitoite

Affirmation: *'I ignite my sacred Merkabah with light languages. I am free from the control of others.'*

35 Violet fire

Transmutation. Detoxification.
Psychic vision. Constant distraction.

35 Violet fire

**Transmutation. Detoxification.
Psychic vision. Constant distraction.**

Sensory abilities are still being understood on scientific terms. Currently perceived limitations of psychic vision and energetic healing restrict your human potential of understanding the communication of the sacred light held by your soul's intelligence.

Holding the sacred fire, the violet flame, the Seventh Ray Master Saint Germaine can easily transmute anxiety and remove and clear negative energy frequencies that are stopping you from listening and hearing your senses accurately in your heart and mind. The violet ray vibration creates freedom and general transmutation.

Calling in the flame of violet fire of Saint Germaine can create a path for miracles and awaken hidden abilities that are dormant within you. If you choose to recalibrate with the violet fire of ascension you will become more attuned to your senses, interpreting the world around you in a clear and accurate way that is free from outside influence.

Ascension Master Saint Germaine arrives to assist in the clearing and detoxification process. He suggests that you remove external and introduced stimuli. Self-indulgence will only distance you from understanding what you currently need, placing a fog over your inner vision. Constant distractions deter clear inner vision.

'Sensory perceptions speak quickly. Learn their messages with structural balance.'

– ASCENDED MASTER SAINT GERMAINE

Sacred crystal: iolite

Affirmation: *'I am the violet fire. My psychic vision is clear.'*

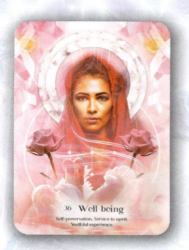

36 Well being

Self-preservation. Service to spirit.
Youthful experience.

36 Well-being

**Self-preservation. Service to spirit.
Youthful experience.**

Personal well-being is a daily task. Freedom from external
disturbance, toxic environments, excessive noise and emotional
chaos need to be acknowledged and addressed if you wish to
achieve a harmonic state of well-being. A peaceful state can be
achieved through a meditative experience, balanced choices
and pure silence, which will give the mind uninterrupted rest.

Ascension Master Lady Nada surrounds herself with
young souls and sacred children, teaching them to connect

to their heart's sensitivity. Time spent with children will increase your joy as you connect to the playful child inside you. Put aside regimented routines and take part in youthful activities to freshen and invigorate your being.

Serving on the Sixth Ray of devotion and service, Lady Nada extends her graceful hands to help your soul find peaceful moments in the chaos of life. When you are at peace harmony will follow, making your mind's intent clear to manifest its desires into reality. Burn any ill feeling with exercise, journalling or meditative practice.

Lady Nada asks that you learn to love those who find it difficult to love themselves. Children and youth need your assistance now. Share and honour your youthful experiences. Seek out peaceful places with water gardens, beaches, country or rainforest to drain the toxicity from your mind and spirit with Lady Nada's assistance.

'Sanction your spirit to the power of silent surrender.'

– *ASCENSION MASTER LADY NADA*

Sacred crystal: white selenite

Affirmation: *'I satisfy my needs with ease. I am at peace.'*

About the author

After being gifted her first tarot deck at 15, Anna began to explore her intuition to understand the psychic messages about people, events and places she experienced during her childhood. Searching to understand her own unique abilities, she found a love for all things paranormal, the ancient past and spiritual connection.

Anna believes her life mission is to educate others about their well-being, spiritual evolution and universal connection through the alchemy of energy medicine. By combining knowledge from our ancient ancestors and conscious self we can rediscover, connect and evolve our soul to create a powerful and meaningful life.

Anna's down-to-earth nature provides compassion, understanding and personal mentoring to students and clients seeking change and transformation. She is a holistic practitioner, certified teacher and reiki master in usui, seichem and Angelic Reiki® and offers intuitive and energetic workshops throughout Australia.

Find out more about Anna at:
annastark.com.au
Facebook: @AnnaStarkAuthor
Instagram: @AnnaStark_Author

About the illustrator

Hailing from Sweden and currently living in Sydney, Australia, Selena Moon has been interested in art, drawing and computers since childhood, and any free subject choices in school always tended towards the creative ones.

She has had her own design studio and years of experience with freelance design work that evolved to include illustrations and digital art. Selena now has an established and successful career as a graphic designer, illustrator and digital artist in both Sweden and Australia.

Her art is a mix of simplicity and bold, colourful pieces. She finds inspiration for her art from various avenues and likes to explore new fields so she doesn't get bound by the same style or technique, utilising her many skills in combination to create unique pieces. As evidenced by this deck, the artworks are an amalgam of digital collage, digital line art and hand-drawn illustrations.

Selena loves nature and, as an immigrant to Australia, finds the surroundings very beautiful and draws inspiration from them. One of the first artworks she created and sold when she came to Australia five years ago was a series of hand-drawn native Australian flowers.

Find out more at hallowedmirror.com or on Instagram: @hallowedmirror

Other publications

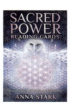

Sacred Power Reading Cards: a transformative guidance for your life journey
ISBN 9781925429275

This 36-card deck will inspire self-empowerment and healing by tapping into sacred symbols and totem animals and delving deep into spiritual realms. This dedicated deck of power symbols will assist you to awaken your spirit's path and open your heart towards new possibilities and guidance.

These cards are also a direct supportive tool for those who work as healing practitioners in any area of emotional and physical well-being modalities such as reiki, kinesiology, counselling, theta healing and more.

Sacred Spirit Reading Cards: spiritual guidance for your life journey
ISBN 9781925682847

Sacred Spirit Reading Cards is a deck of 36 cards of visionary artworks that will help you look beyond the physical realm and connect to higher vibrational energies to empower your spirit with confidence and direct you towards positive life paths.

A supportive tool for professional therapists, well-being modalities and healing practitioners in all areas of energy medicine, these cards will uplift your spirit and soul and help awaken your higher self so you can create clear celestial connections for inner guidance.